THE OFFICIAL GUIDE TO TAX RESOLUTION

THE OFFICIAL GUIDE TO TAX RESOLUTION

HOW TO USE THE IRS RULEBOOK TO YOUR ADVANTAGE

JOE AGUILAR

America's Tax Resolution Referee™

THE OFFICIAL GUIDE TO TAX RESOLUTION
How to Use the IRS Rulebook to Your Advantage

Copyright © 2023 Joe Aguilar
All rights reserved.

Paperback ISBN: 978-1-956220-90-2
eBook ISBN: 978-1-956220-91-9

Expert
Press
www.ExpertPress.net

Editing by Michael Hume
Copyediting by Lori Price
Text design and composition by Emily Fritz
Cover design by Casey Fritz

CONTENTS

INTRODUCTION

THE PROBLEM AND THE SOLUTION

If you're reading this book, chances are it's because you have a tax problem. Maybe you owe a substantial amount of back taxes to the IRS but don't know where to turn. Maybe you have been ignoring the notices they send you hoping your problem will somehow just disappear.

A colleague once reminded me of the old phrase, "Bad news doesn't get better with age." In other words, ignoring your tax problem will not make it go away.

There are plenty of ways people get into tax problems. Here are just a few:

- They don't report all—or any!—of their income.

- They make mathematical errors in their calculations.

- They live beyond their means.

- They don't have enough money deducted from their paychecks.

- They claim tax credits they should not have claimed.

- They claim dependents they should not have claimed.

- They don't report inheritance and other taxable assets.

The people who have tax problems like these all have something in common. They broke the IRS rules. They didn't know, didn't understand, didn't care, or maybe even chose to ignore the IRS rules. So now they have a problem. And that's why they need me.

I'm a rules kind of guy. I'm a retired Marine, and you don't get far in the Marine Corps without knowing the rules. I've also been a referee for more than twenty years. I referee professional and collegiate volleyball all over the US. I know the volleyball rulebook inside and out, and I know how to apply the rules fairly and honestly for both teams.

I also know the IRS rulebook inside and out, and that's why I'm a Tax Resolution Referee.

I'm Joe—America's Tax Resolution Referee™.

I'm your referee: someone who knows the rules and will apply them to reach a resolution in your favor. I am America's Tax Resolution Referee™. I am the tax expert who will use his knowledge to help you resolve your tax problem fairly, accurately, and ethically. I will take a non-biased and honest approach to your tax issue; I will review your plays (tax documents) and make the calls (offers) that are fair and based on your individual skills and playing history (income and assets). I will review the entire situation so we can make the right call based on your situation.

Some people resist using a tax expert. Why? Maybe they don't trust anyone to help them with their tax problem. Maybe they believe they can do it themselves. Maybe they think tax help is too expensive. I will not take your case if I cannot help you.

When people tell me they can do it themselves, I show them this IRS Taxpayer Roadmap.

The roadmap, for all its complexity, only scratches the surface of the IRS rulebook. That's why you need a tax expert. That's why you need someone like me. I take my Tax Resolution Referee status seriously. I'll abide by the IRS rulebook, but I'll also help make the rules work for you.

IRS TAYPAYER ROADMAP

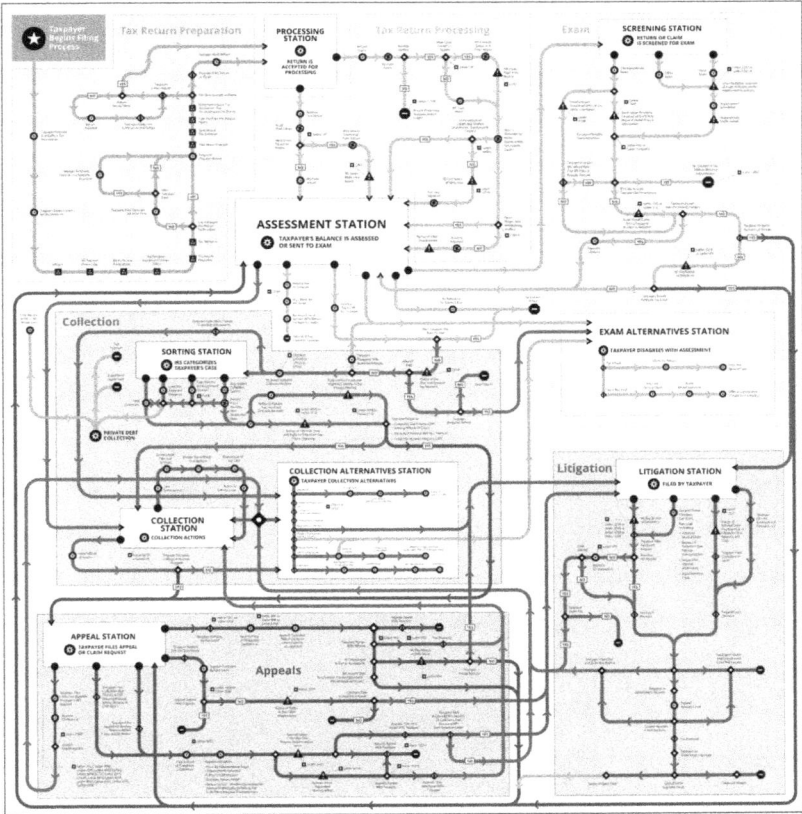

https://www.taxpayeradvocate.irs.gov/get-help/roadmap/

CHAPTER 1

THE MAKING
OF A REFEREE

1

I wasn't always a tax referee who helped people solve tax problems. After high school, I thought I wanted to play football for the University of Colorado. I moved from California to Colorado, but after a while, I figured out that it was not a good fit. I still wanted an education, so I called 1-800-MARINES and joined the Corps.

Two months later, I left for Marine Corps boot camp. My military experience changed my life forever. While on active duty, I was stationed in Okinawa, Japan, and also went to college there. In college, I took an auditing class instructed by someone who worked at the Marine Corps Nonappropriated Fund Audit Service. They were impressed by my performance in the class and invited me to join their specialized group. Soon after, I became an internal auditor for the Marine Corps, a job I held for six years. In the meantime, I earned degrees in accounting and business management. Eventually, they closed the auditing field to active duty, so I was sent back to the Fleet Marine Corps, then on to multiple deployments, eventually joining the Marine Corps Recruiting Station in Orange County, Caifornia.

While traveling the Pacific and networking all over the West Coast, I was allowed to grow my part-time tax preparation business into a full-time endeavor. The incident that sealed my fate and interest involved my family: My father was in trouble with the IRS. He could not sell his home because the IRS was going to take everything. I decided to help my dad with his tax issue, and I was able to resolve it.

Shortly after this win, a new client walked into my Tustin, California, office. He was being audited by the IRS. At the time, I was not licensed to represent before the IRS, but the client was desperate for help and was impressed by my level of knowledge. He realized I was good at taxes and accounting and begged me to help him win his case. I studied the tax rules, reviewed his specialized situation, and went to the audit with him. Collaboratively, we saved more than $100,000 that the IRS said he owed. The client was ecstatic. And I was pumped.

After those two back-to-back experiences, my confidence grew, and I committed to becoming a tax resolution powerhouse. I studied the tax laws, learned all I could, and got my Enrolled Agent (EA) license.

I first started doing taxes because I was broke. After my divorce, I needed more money to support my four boys, so I started working in the evenings as a part-time tax preparer. I started with H&R Block, but I didn't like upselling products to people who didn't need them. I was tired of meeting quotas; I wanted to help people without the pressure of selling them products they didn't need. Because I still loved playing volleyball and wanted to stay involved in that part of my life, I started officiating volleyball on the weekends while I worked at my tax prep business during the week. I am fortunate to referee at the Division 1 level in both men's and women's volleyball and also on various beach and indoor pro tours.

You might think my twin passions of officiating volleyball and working in tax resolution are wildly different, but you would be surprised at how much they have in common. In both instances, my role is to know the rulebook inside and out and then apply the rules honestly and fairly.

Fast forward to today. I finally feel at home. I decided to transition from tax preparation to full-time tax resolution. I handle my first love—tax resolution clients—full time, and I referee volleyball on weekends. I am living the dream. I am helping my clients resolve their tax issues, and I'm doing what I was meant to do. Every day, I help people who need my assistance. Every day I help them win. I teach them, apply complicated tax rules to their situation, and facilitate the plays so they can win.

WHAT MAKES ME AND MY FIRM STAND OUT

Tax guys and dentists have a bad rap—sort of like the IRS. People put off getting their teeth fixed until they have a problem. People aren't proactive about dental work or taxes because they just don't want to deal with them. People who come to me have real issues and need workable solutions.

I'm different from most tax resolution professionals. Over nearly twenty years, I have acquired specialized knowledge and learned how to handle specific tax-related situations. I know how to apply the rules fairly. I always lay out all the information so my clients can see and understand it. I present them with a plan to resolve their problem that is based on the rules and facts, not based on some arbitrary number, but on actual financials, using real-life math and numbers. I understand how to look at every tax situation, identify the applicable rules, and determine how I can help.

My license is specialized, focusing on taxes. Others have a general license in accountancy—like a CPA—and tax lawyers who can also practice before the IRS. I study the rules and regulations closely. I stay abreast of issues that might impact my clients negatively. Although I can prepare a regular return and often help clients with theirs, that's not my focus.

HOW DO I DETERMINE WHETHER I CAN HELP?

No, I don't help everyone. I help people when I can provide a benefit. I want them to know they're going to get a fair deal with me. If I can't provide you with a benefit, then I'm not going to let you hire me. If someone isn't going to get a benefit, I let them know, and I don't take their money. Otherwise, I use the IRS rulebook to figure out how I can help them.

We start with a Thirty Minute Tax Resolution Strategy Meeting. There's no charge for this meeting. Here are some documents I'll want to review:

- The IRS's tax liability assessment

- Tax returns

- The client's assets (home, cars, property, etc.)

- Amount owed to the IRS

- Amount owed on client's house and other properties

- Current and future income

I'll review all of this information to see if I can help. I am an honest tax expert. I'm not going to go to work for someone unless I know I have a high chance of success in resolving their tax problem. I'm not here to just take people's money. I'm here to do a job—a good job.

By the end of our thirty-minute meeting, I'll know whether I can help this client. If I

I WILL SHOW YOU WITH MY ACTIONS THAT I'M HERE FOR YOU.

see that I can help, the client will leave the meeting with a roadmap for resolving their tax issue and one all-inclusive price.

Just like my job in volleyball, I'm a referee. I'm going to let the game happen, but I'm going to oversee it. The only difference is that, unlike in volleyball, I'm not impartial. I care who wins. We're going to do whatever we need to do to win.

I'm not going to say I'll call you every other day or that you're my only client, because that's not true. However, I will show you with my actions that I'm here for you. I'm supportive; I do what I say I'll do. I'll do my best to help you reach your goals.

I only take on clients I can help. If I can't help you—or if you don't need me—I will tell you so immediately, just like I told Jack.

JACK'S STORY

A while ago, I talked to someone about our services. I'll call him Jack. He decided not to sign up then, but since he was still on my leads list, I called him later and asked him again if we could help. He said, "I took care of my '20 and '21 returns. I just need help with the other four." Jack then told me he was not self-employed and wanted me to go back to 2016 because he had read he needed to do six years of returns. This is where my experience comes in. Yes, he was right that he needed to go back six years, but it was November 2022 when I talked to him. So, six years would now be 2016–2021.

We were not going to add 2016, because it was almost the end of the year. It made sense not to include it unless he had qualified for some type of offer or agreement with the IRS. But because it was so close to the end of the year, did he need to go back to 2016 or start with 2017? Did he really need six years done? Did he have any substitute for returns that needed to be replaced with real returns? He told us he received refunds for 2021 and 2020. I thought, *Dude, just do 2022 and move on with life.* In this case, he would not qualify for a refund for older returns because he had three years from the date it was due.

I told him, "You don't need me. Go ahead and finish that tax return. You're done. Then walk away from this whole thing." And he said, "Really, dude?" I said, "Yeah." He thanked me for my honesty, and I told him, "No problem."

Sometimes, though, I meet a client I just can't help. For example, let me tell you about Clyde.

CLYDE'S STORY

Clyde came to me recently because he was being audited. Unfortunately, he didn't hire me until after he had done the initial meeting with the IRS by himself. I looked at the auditor's notes from that initial meeting, and all I could tell him was he needed to pay the bill and keep his mouth shut. That's it. I couldn't get him out of it. He set himself up for failure with the things he said in the meeting.

They asked him about his education, and he told them he had an MBA. The auditor asked, "So you understand finance? You've had a business for nine years and have never reported any income, but you're taking the expenses every year?"

Clyde is a disc jockey. He loves being a DJ, but he doesn't make any money at it. The auditor asked, "Why do you do this if you don't get paid?" Clyde told her how much he enjoyed the work and that he had been trying to get his name out there as a DJ. Logically enough, the auditor asked whether he would do the work for free, and Clyde told her he would because he enjoyed it so much. That's when the auditor broke the news to him: "You do not have a business. You have a hobby."

He basically took a shotgun to his own foot. When I was reviewing the notes, I almost couldn't believe what I was reading. The auditor only examined two years. One of those years, Clyde wrote off $49,000 in business expenses; in the other, he wrote off $51,000. He was lucky the auditor didn't decide to open a third year and add yet another $49,000 in taxable income, plus all the penalties and interest carried forward.

He didn't tell me he had been writing off business expenses for nine years without reporting any income.

By the time Clyde got done shooting himself in the foot during his IRS meeting, there was literally nothing I could do for him except tell him to pay his bill and be thankful he got off as easily as he did.

Clients like Clyde are frustrating because I can't help them. But there's nothing better than being able to resolve a client's tax problem and relieve their stress. For instance, let me tell you about Bob.

BOB'S STORY

Bob came to me owing the IRS $207,621. I managed to get him an Offer in Compromise (OIC) for $119.00. But then the IRS found out he had paid my firm $5,000, and they tried to raise the settlement price by another $5,000 because they believed he had more money. I called the officer on Bob's case. I asked what would happen if we disagreed with the increase in offer amount, and she said that might cause the whole offer to be rejected. Then I talked to Bob, who said that given how much money I had already saved him, he would find a way to make the extra $5,000 work.

We agreed to the adjustment, but we didn't hear anything back. A week went by, then two. I called the officer back multiple times because she said she was sending me the adjusted offer, but I had not received it. She finally called back after a week and a half to tell us she had reconsidered the numbers and thought we were right. The IRS couldn't just change the offer without a good reason. She made some adjustments to her notes, and five or six weeks later, she called back to say they had accepted the original offer at $119.00. In addition to saving over $200,000 with the IRS, we also got an offer through with the state of California saving him over $50,000 in state taxes.

This is what makes my job so much fun. I love helping people save money with the IRS.

CHAPTER 2

COMMON
TAX PROBLEMS

2

Tax relief is what my firm and I are all about. In the introduction, I shared some of the reasons people get into tax problems. But what, exactly, can happen to you if you fail to pay your taxes on time? These are just a few of the most common problems. We can help with any of them.

WAGE GARNISHMENT

When you have a tax problem, the IRS doesn't start by issuing a wage garnishment—an order to your employer to deduct money from your paycheck to pay your debt. They start by using other, less aggressive forms of collection, such as mailing you notices. By statute—the IRS's rulebook—they have to exhaust all of these options without success before they can garnish your wages. But if you've been ignoring the IRS letters and notices, your case could arrive at the point where the IRS has no other choice but to garnish your wages. If your tax debt case reaches that point, you need a professional's help. In volleyball terms, a wage garnishment is a hard spike by the IRS!

BANK (OR PROPERTY) LEVY

Another collection provision in the IRS's rulebook is the ability to simply seize (or "levy") the money in your bank account and take and sell any of your other property (i.e., real estate, vehicles, or any personal property in your name) to satisfy your tax debt. This is another of the IRS's most aggressive collection tools (another hard spike), and again, they don't start by simply seizing your assets. By the time your bank account has been levied, you've received multiple notices from the IRS informing you that you have a tax problem. When you get an IRS letter titled "Final Notice of Intent to Levy," that's exactly what it says it is: It's your last warning before your property is seized. If your case reaches this point, you immediately need professional tax help in order to understand your rights according to the rulebook. Contact any *Eagle Tax Resolution* office right away at 888-EAGLE-05. (Our direct lines and local contact details are included at the back of the book.)

THREATENING LETTERS

The IRS has little to no interest in your personal affairs. Their interest is purely in collecting the tax you owe. Once they determine (or suspect) that you owe a debt you haven't paid, they'll start sending you threatening letters. These are not empty threats on the part of the IRS, so ignoring them is something you do at your own peril. But there's no need to panic. These letters are not the IRS's way of spiking the ball down your throat. In volleyball terms, these are just "serves"—believe it or not, they don't want to get aggressive with you. They want to close your case. Open any correspondence you get from the IRS. Read the notices carefully. Look for errors; for example, if you have already sent your payment, you should "return the ball" immediately by contacting the IRS to tell them so. The sooner you start addressing your tax problem, the better things will go for your case.

IRS AUDIT NOTIFICATION

If you receive an audit letter from the IRS, without a doubt, it's scary and nerve-wracking. But the first step is not to panic. Letters like these are simply the way the IRS communicates with taxpayers—they aren't

THE SOONER YOU START ADDRESSING YOUR TAX PROBLEM, THE BETTER THINGS WILL GO FOR YOUR CASE.

always meant to be threatening or alarming. They are just the IRS's way of telling you they suspect a problem exists and need to resolve it. They aren't "spiking the ball" yet; think of the audit letter as a preparatory "set," but be aware that the spike may be coming! For most taxpayers, the best next step is to contact a tax resolution professional like *Eagle Tax Resolution*, who will help you fully understand the audit process and meet all the IRS's deadlines. Get your team to the net to be ready for whatever the IRS hurls at you next.

NON-FILING

For individual taxpayers, failing to file a tax return is one of the worst possible errors in the eyes of the IRS. It's like not even showing up for the big match. In fact, most people don't know that the penalties for *not filing* a return are much stiffer than the penalties for filing and *not paying* the tax on time. Failing to file doesn't make the debt go away!

When your business fails to file its taxes, the IRS may simply issue a substitute return for you, the business owner. This will not save you money—in fact, it will very likely cost your business much more than if you'd filed your return in the first place. Do you really want the IRS to compute your taxes? They will not include any of the allowable deductions a qualified tax professional will include. A substitute return will only include your income. If the IRS issues a substitute return, you will definitely end up with a higher tax liability than if you filed on time.

PROPERTY LIENS

Similar to a levy, the IRS rulebook allows them to put a federal tax lien on your real estate, vehicles, or personal property. In legal terms, the lien is in favor of the United States and grants the government the right to seize your property to be sold to satisfy your tax debt. In volleyball terms, it's akin to your opponent simply keeping the ball and not allowing you to play at all! That's because, even though they haven't yet seized your property—technically, you still own it—you can't sell it until the tax lien is removed. Your *Eagle Tax Resolution* professional can help you with a game plan to respond to a tax lien if one is issued against your property.

"INNOCENT SPOUSE"

Because there are benefits allowed by the practice, married couples often choose to file joint tax returns. Both spouses are then *jointly and individually* responsible for payment of the taxes and any interest and penalties associated with the tax debt. What happens when a divorce occurs? Even if a divorce decree makes one of the spouses responsible for all amounts owed on previous joint returns, the other spouse could still be stuck with the bill, even if they weren't the main income earner. Imagine being a star volleyball player, maybe a specialist in spiking the ball, but turning around to find the rest of your team had walked away and left you to battle the opponents alone! The IRS offers three types of relief for cases like this: Innocent Spouse Relief, Separation of Liability, and Equitable Relief. In some cases, the innocent spouse can be relieved of the tax, interest, and penalties resulting from a joint return. Your Tax Resolution Referee can help you navigate the rulebook if you find yourself in the "innocent spouse" situation.

PENALTIES AND INTEREST

While your tax debt remains outstanding, the meter is still running on penalties and interest owed on your debt. The longer you wait to address the problem, the bigger the problem gets! It's as if your team hasn't made it out of the locker room, but your opponents are allowed to keep serving the ball to your empty side of the court and scoring points in your absence. By the time your team shows up, you're in a deeper hole than you would otherwise be in. Get help from the referee right away.

CHAPTER 3

CAN YOU RESOLVE TAX PROBLEMS ON YOUR OWN?

3

Depending on your unique situation, you could do your taxes on your own or even handle your own tax resolution case. You could look up things and try to figure out your tax situation yourself. You may succeed, and you may not. However, if you don't succeed, you could get into a lot of trouble, leading to even bigger tax issues, more money owed, and other financial problems. So why wouldn't you want help from an expert?

A good volleyball team wouldn't try to play without a coach, especially if they can get a coach who's also a referee. I've helped thousands of clients with their resolutions. I'm the Tax Resolution Referee™, but I understand there are several reasons why clients choose not to use our services. Here are the three most common reasons I hear:

1   **They don't trust the process** or have had so many bad experiences in the past that they don't trust anyone. Maybe they responded to one of the many ads offered by a so-called nationwide tax resolution firm, paid that firm $300 a month (or more), and had bad results (or no results at all). It would be no surprise if they no longer trust tax professionals. The issue with this is that the previous "expert" probably didn't put more than an hour's worth of work into trying to help the taxpayer. Often, the "experts" at these national firms operate much like a volleyball coach who has his team bat the ball around for an hour, call that "practice," and then leave them to figure out the rest on the court during a key match. I would never operate that way. I put *way more* effort into your case. In fact, if I can help you—if I take on your tax

resolution case—there's no limit to what I'll do to legitimately and legally help you win.

2 **They think they can do it themselves.** They read a few tax resolution books or watch a few videos, and they think they're ready to take on the IRS. Spoiler alert: They're definitely not! Do you think you and your teammates could read a book about volleyball or watch a match on television and run out and take on the defending champs without having played the game? That's what this "do-it-yourself" strategy often amounts to. This is your first tax resolution case. Your opponents (the IRS) have played the game thousands of times. Believe me, the likelihood that you can be successful going it alone, especially if your situation has any unusual aspects, is almost zero. The good news is that I have also played the game many times, and I know what your opponents know, along with understanding the

rulebook inside and out. Wouldn't you want me on your team when the big match comes up?

3 **They don't think they need the service** because they previously bought a "peace of mind" package from one of the big firms. Unfortunately, with these services, you typically pay about $200, and you get an inexperienced person to try to help

you. The big companies offering these services hire inexperienced agents who often don't know what they're doing. It's like paying a rookie who's never played the game a pro's salary and expecting them to perform like the pro, but they simply aren't.

I have an answer for all of these folks. When you have a problem with the IRS—whatever the problem, whatever the reason—call me. Once you hire me, you don't have to deal directly with the IRS at all. It should go without saying that your "team" should include seasoned professionals, like those at *Eagle Tax Resolution*, who know the rulebook inside and out and who know how to play the tax resolution game to win.

* * *

No matter what your IRS opponents are doing to collect on your tax debt, you're bound to be in the grip of some serious emotions, especially fear. You will not perform at your best when you're operating from a place of fear. From the first scary IRS letter to the receipt of a Final Notice of Intent to Levy, all of the opponent's moves can be extremely intimidating and can quickly put you back on your heels (emotionally speaking).

That said, the IRS notice that most often strikes fear in the heart of a taxpayer is the dreaded audit letter. So let's talk about audits next.

IT SHOULD GO WITHOUT SAYING THAT YOUR "TEAM" SHOULD INCLUDE SEASONED PROFESSIONALS.

CHAPTER 4

ALL ABOUT AUDITS

4

An income tax audit is a close review by the IRS of an individual's or business's past tax returns for discrepancies. The IRS's computer system routinely reviews financial information for income and deduction authenticity, and when it finds something weird, it flags the taxpayer's return as "abnormal." Once the IRS system triggers a review, a more thorough examination of financial information and accounts will be completed by an experienced auditor.

THREE TYPES OF IRS AUDITS

Depending on the nature of the abnormality triggered by the computer system, the IRS will conduct their audit by one of three different methods: by mail, in person at their office, or in person at your home or place of business (a "field" audit).

- **The mail audit** is the easiest of the three audit types for the IRS representative and the taxpayer. No meetings need to be scheduled. The IRS simply asks for information you can submit by mail, and you can receive their findings by mail.

- **The IRS office audit** requires the taxpayer (you) to schedule a time to visit the local IRS office and meet in person with the auditor for a more thorough examination of your financial situation. In the case of an office audit, you'll need to bring everything you need to make your case, from personal or business bank statements to records related to your "allowable expenses" (such as your car payment and mortgage or rent payment). When an office audit is scheduled, the IRS permits you to bring an authorized representative

BEING AUDITED OFTEN RESULTS IN BIG PROBLEMS, ESPECIALLY IF THERE IS FRAUDULENT BEHAVIOUR INVOLVED.

(attorney, CPA, or Enrolled Agent) along with you.

- This is an excellent provision; you are far less likely to get a favorable audit outcome if you go it alone. Don't set foot on the court without a coach! And if you want the best result, take a coach who thoroughly understands the game and the rulebook. You know who to call.

- **A field audit** is the trickiest type of audit to "survive." It's the IRS's most intensive type of audit. They'll often call for a field audit if they're questioning more than one of the deductions you've claimed. In many cases, they will review every single item on your return. For instance, are you claiming rent and utilities for your business? During a field audit, the auditor will want to inspect your office. To be a legitimate deduction for total rent and utilities, it cannot be a home office. That is a different deduction. A home office has to be a space in your home used exclusively for your business. Most people hear that a home office will trigger an audit, and that is simply not true. Much of the time it's because people report all of their rent and utilities on a Schedule C as an expense. The home office worksheet allows a portion based on the total square footage of the home to be used as exclusive office space. I have seen many who have deducted their entire rent or mortgage and utilities as business expenses.

AN AUDIT WILL REVEAL ANY DISHONESTY

Being audited often results in big problems, especially if there is fraudulent behaviour involved.

I had a client once who was involved with a fraudulent business. They were writing off expenses to reduce their overall income. They got caught. Even though they were in the wrong, I was able to help.

I called the auditor and told them I could agree that my client's business was not legitimate. "A lot of people make mistakes," I said. I let the auditor know I had already explained the rules to my client about how to approach these issues going forward, and I understood that the IRS would nevertheless need to assess a penalty. But this is a good example of why "coming clean" can really help your relationship with the IRS. Instead of assessing the typical 10 percent penalty, in this case, I asked for a 6 percent penalty. Because my client was now in compliance, the auditor was willing to grant the penalty reduction.

This is why professionals need to be hired in these cases. I know what I'm talking about, and I know what to say (and what not to say) to the IRS. I'm able to see every case from its unique perspective and act accordingly. It's like having badly behaved children. Based on the type of their bad behavior and their reaction to being caught, you're going to discipline them differently. The IRS doesn't really want to bring out the heavy hammers, but they will do so if they perceive a taxpayer has given them no alternative. When they have a case with a taxpayer who is clearly dealing with them in an above-board manner (and especially when that taxpayer has engaged the services of a true tax resolution professional), they're typically much more willing to meet them halfway where they can.

I come from an audit background. I was an internal auditor. So I know how to think like an auditor, and I know how to deal with these cases. I can think like a good IRS auditor is going to think, trying to put themselves in the client's mind.

Another of my clients brought in tax returns that were so wrong—practically fraudulent—that we needed to start fresh. He had claimed many business expenses, but he had zero revenue. The IRS takes the justifiable position that if you're not selling anything, you don't actually have a business. The expenses this client was trying to claim were "start-up costs," not true business write-offs, and he hadn't actually claimed any revenue for four years. You can't write off expenses for four years because you say you're *planning* on going into business.

The IRS uses a tool called BizStats (www.bizstats.com), and since it's available publicly, our staff jumped onto BizStats to check the legitimacy of the client's claims in exactly the same way the IRS would. The client told me he had paid out $10,000 in commissions. Commissions on what? When we pulled up the information on the client's industry, we found this industry typically pays a 3 percent commission on *sales.* So, it was easy enough to do the math the same way the IRS would: $10,000 in commissions at 3 percent meant the client had to have had $427,000 in sales. Of course the IRS would question his return. Why would he pay commissions if he had no sales?

If you show me a tax return, my staff is going to look at it. Thoroughly. We're going to tell you upfront if it's going to raise red flags with the IRS—and particularly if it is, in fact,

BS. If your return is not going to fly, or if it's likely to get you audited, we can usually help you fix it before it's too late.

HOW TO REDUCE YOUR CHANCES OF BEING AUDITED

Here are the best practices you can implement to give your tax filings the best chance of avoiding the type of IRS scrutiny that could result in a problematic audit:

1. Hire someone who knows what they're doing to assist you in preparing your tax filing. Not all EAs, CPAs, or lawyers are created equal! Check reviews!

2. Keep good records so you can substantiate any expenses.

3. File taxes on time and avoid amending returns.

4. Provide details and more details.

5. Do not overvalue expenses and donated goods.

6. Avoid taking excessive deductions.

7. Do not underreport income.

8. Check your math and make sure no discrepancies exist.

9. Don't forget to sign your returns.

WHAT HAPPENS WHEN YOU GET THE DREADED IRS LETTER

The IRS sends many different types of letters, so the first thing to do is understand the type of letter you've received. One common letter is a notice the IRS has found a discrepancy between what's on your return and what has been reported to them (e.g., money taken from a retirement account, mismatches in income versus fees reported by a business, etc.).

Another common IRS letter points out inaccuracies the IRS has perceived in your return. That's not an audit . . . it's simply a notice that they found a discrepancy. The IRS has information on you in their system; if what you report to them differs from what they have in their system, they'll want to review everything to see where the mistake is. The IRS makes mistakes, too, so this review could actually be a chance for you to rectify *their* error.

Letters with a code starting with "CP" means they're "Computer Paragraph" findings. These letters indicate the IRS's computer system found some type of mismatch.

When you get any type of letter from the IRS, your best next step is to contact someone who knows their way around the different letters and can clarify for you what's going on, what the IRS is likely looking for. Call us.

Bad news does not get better with time. Ignoring these letters from the IRS is your WORST option. It's a little like a volleyball player getting called for a fault and continuing to commit that same fault over and over.

Not a good idea!

CHAPTER 5

ALL ABOUT OFFERS

5

When you have an unpaid tax debt, you find yourself in a serious match against the IRS. Since a tax problem can have a significant negative impact on you and your family, and since its resolution can affect your finances for many years (or the rest of your life), you must play to win. You're playing for the championship! You're going to need a coach who's also a referee because "winning" will be defined as reaching an outcome that is fair to both sides of the "net." And the *offer* your Tax Resolution Referee might be able to make to the IRS on your behalf will establish the parameters of this all-important showdown.

The IRS rulebook (the "Internal Revenue Manual") (IRM) provides for a program called the "Offer In Compromise" (OIC). This program is the primary tool available for resolving an otherwise-insoluble tax problem. The OIC program allows *qualified* taxpayers to negotiate a settlement with the IRS to pay an amount that is less than the amount they originally owed on their tax debt. In general, it's simple: Based on your true financial situation, you make an offer to the IRS that you can live with. If they accept your offer, you're off the hook once you've honored your end of the bargain and paid the agreed-upon settlement amount.

It's simple in general, but many details make each offer something that has to be carefully crafted based on the taxpayer's circumstances. It's important to know that the IRS turns down the overwhelming majority of offers it receives, and an understanding of how the IRS evaluates your offer is crucial if you want to be one of the relative handful of tax debtors whose offer is accepted.

AT EAGLE TAX RESOLUTION, WE TAKE A VERY DIFFERENT APPROACH.

"OFFER MILLS"

Why does the IRS reject the overwhelming majority of offers with which they're presented—at least 80 percent by most estimates?

The answer is that the overwhelming majority of offers the IRS receives come from large, nationally-advertised "tax resolution" firms, which are essentially nothing more than "offer mills." They are in the business of convincing people with tax problems to engage their services so they can make an offer to the IRS on their behalf. They're basically salespeople. They'll collect nothing more than basic information from you (including your Social Security number), along with your payment for their services. Then they'll throw together an offer they may well know has little chance of being accepted. And they don't care.[1]

They're not *really* in the tax resolution business. Their primary focus is not on

---

1   See IRS News Release IR-2023-63, dated March 30, 2023, titled Dirty Dozen: Watch out for Offer in Compromise "mills" where promoters claim their services are needed to settle IRS debts.

whether their clients get the best possible outcome in their championship match against the IRS—they are focused on "selling" offers. They're not going to take the time to make sure a client is truly qualified to make an acceptable offer to the IRS. They typically won't dig into the many details to determine whether or not an offer will "fly." And that's why most of their offers are rejected.

At *Eagle Tax Resolution,* we take a very different approach. We don't sell offers. We dig into a client's real financial situation, and we tell you upfront whether we think you'll qualify for an offer.

If the answer is no, we'll tell you right away and look for other ways to help you get the IRS monkey off your back over whatever time that takes.

But if the answer is yes, we'll put together an offer we know you can live with—which we're confident the IRS will accept—because it will be an offer that's fair to "both sides of the net." Even if we accept your case based on what you've told us, our staff will do the necessary due diligence to learn whether you really are qualified for an OIC. In a sense, our staff will try to *disqualify* you, looking for important details you didn't mention to us upfront, but which the IRS will definitely uncover when they consider any offer. If our staff can't find a reason to disqualify you, we'll proceed with the offer.

That's why, despite the fact the IRS rejects more than 80 percent of the offers it receives overall, our track record at *Eagle Tax Resolution* is very different. Once we make an offer, based on our statistical history, it stands better than a *95 percent* chance of IRS acceptance.

THE CLOCK IS RUNNING

By statute, the IRS has ten years, and ten years only, to collect the tax debt you owe. The clock starts running when you file a return for which you don't then pay the tax bill. (This is another reason it's important to *file* your return on time, even if you can't *pay* on time.)

This collection statute is one of the key factors in determining whether the IRS will accept your OIC. It forms the boundaries of the IRS's collection efforts, much like the lines on the volleyball court define what is inbounds and what is out of bounds.

If you have the ability to pay your tax debt within those boundaries—before the "Collection Statute Expiration Date" (CSED) when the clock runs out on the IRS—you will have to pay your debt in full. But if the IRS is presented with a strong case that you will not be able to pay the full debt before the CSED, your OIC has a good chance of being accepted.

There are factors that could extend, or "toll," this collection period, such as changes in your circumstances, failure to file on time, or failure to make payments you agreed to make. That's why we take great pains to make sure your offer is not only acceptable to the IRS, but is something you can live with and represents payments you can make *without fail.*

BASIC QUALIFICATIONS FOR OIC

To qualify for an OIC, the taxpayer needs to have:

- filed all tax returns.

- received a tax bill for at least one period.

- made all required estimated tax payments for the current year.

Beyond that, the IRS has to be presented with a strong case that shows not only can't you pay your tax debt now, but you don't have the potential to earn enough to pay the full debt before the CSED.

REDUCING YOUR TAX LIABILITY

Before we make an offer to pay what the IRS says you owe, we sometimes have the ability to ask for an "instant replay" of sorts and go back to amend your return so you don't owe as much as the IRS originally believed. If this is possible in your case, we'll want to do everything we can to make sure we're resolving your *true* and fair tax debt. It could be that you owed less, and you really could afford to pay off the debt and get on with your life. When appropriate, I'll always advise clients to take a strong look at whether or not their original return was correct and some adjustments could be made to reduce their overall tax liability.

Does that mean all my clients will take my advice? No, they won't. Some clients choose other options, and although I would like them to take my advice, I always respect their decision regardless of the outcome.

For instance, let me tell you about a client I'll call June. She came to see me because she owed the IRS money she couldn't pay. June didn't have any assets other than her house. I reviewed a few of June's past tax returns, and I immediately saw some errors in the accounting. There were several deductions she should have taken but didn't. For example, she has a disabled adult child in her home, and the state was paying her to care for her adult child, which made part of the income received nontaxable.

I told June we could fix the return so that she would owe less. But she hesitated because she had taken her returns to one of those large nationally-advertised "offer mill" firms, and they had told her the returns were correct. I told her they were wrong, that I could see where the problems were. In my mind, it was a relatively straightforward solution to June's tax problem. It was clear as day to me. But not to June.

Running on emotions and fear, June seemed afraid to trust me to help her. She didn't see any way out of her mess besides selling her house to pay the higher (incorrect) tax bill. June didn't listen to me but instead consulted her kids, who also didn't see any other possibilities and advised her to sell the house. She made an emotional decision out of fear.

June sold her home, and the IRS took all of the profits from the sale. She could have taken advantage of our services at *Eagle Tax Resolution,* but opted against it. She did not need an OIC because her taxes were wrong. We could have fixed it, but instead June decided not to fight back at all—not to even return her opponents' serve!—and she ended up losing big.

EVERY CASE IS DIFFERENT

My firm takes care to review every individual client's needs and to create a plan that works for them. No two cases are the same. When I'm going to bat for someone who owes $1,000,000, there are things I'll do differently from what I'll do if I'm dealing with a case that has landed in the IRS's Automated Collections System (ACS) for $20,000. It's a different give-and-take. I can't always promise the client will get whatever they want because I have to respect the government's interest as well as the client's. But no matter what, I'm going to do my best to keep money in their pocket.

My job is to figure out where and how I can save you money on taxes. If I can get you an offer, I will get you an offer. If I can't get you an offer, I'm going to tell you in our initial meeting. I'll tell you straight-out if I know you're not qualified. I won't lie to you.

I consider the government's needs and my client's needs when making resolution offers. But the IRS has a duty to be fair, too.

If they're going to go after someone for $100,000, but the taxpayer doesn't have $100,000 to give, then there's a problem on both sides of the "net." I'll negotiate for a fair deal that follows the rulebook—in this case, the Internal Revenue Manual (IRM)— and what is fair for both sides. And every case is different.

Let's say we have a client who doesn't make enough money to pay their full tax debt before the end of the collection statute. I could try to drag things out, which could cause the IRS to spend a lot of money on collections, or I could just make a fair offer upfront. I often choose the latter. I want clients to know I'm going to be fair and reasonable. I'm going to tell the IRS exactly what you make, how many assets you have, and any extenuating circumstances they should consider.

I get OICs accepted when I file them because I'm honest. I do my due diligence beforehand. I make offers that make financial sense. I make offers that get accepted. And, if I can't, I don't make the offer.

THE IRS WON'T IGNORE FUTURE EARNING POTENTIAL

I told somebody recently they were not qualified for an offer. The guy owed $200,000. I reviewed his assets, and he had enough at his disposal to cover the liability. He claimed he didn't make enough due to a recent drop in his income. I reviewed his files and discovered he made $400,000 two years ago and $300,000 three years ago. Although his income is far less now ($30,000) and his business shut down due to the pandemic, the IRS doesn't expect him to stay at a low income. They will evaluate his case based on his earning history and future earning potential. They know he isn't going to stay living at that low wage, so they won't accept a lowball offer.

I told him it's not feasible to make a low offer. I told him I understood that he has bills and expenses, but the IRS has expectations.

They know he typically lives at a certain level and assume he will continue to live at that level or higher in the future.

LIVING ABOVE YOUR MEANS

Another client I worked with wanted a good offer based on his inability to pay. The problem was he owned two vehicles. First of all, the IRS only allows for you to pay for one vehicle when you owe them money. His payments were $2,000 a month, but the standard allowed was only $500 (it's currently $625). He was "broke," but only because he was paying substantially over the standard. So when I took those payments down to $500, he had $1,500 left over every month. Based on the standards and the allowable expenses, he could make payments to the IRS of up to $1,500 a month.

Because of this, I know the IRS would not accept his offer. But if he had gone to someone less experienced, they might have taken a quick look at the numbers and told him he could apply for an offer because he was in the negative. They would submit it, and then it would be rejected.

MAKING AN UNACCEPTABLE OFFER HAS CONSEQUENCES

So what? So what if I have an offer mill make an offer that might be turned down by the IRS? Even if there's a small chance they might overlook some details and accept my lowball offer, isn't it worthwhile to try?

No.

You'll suffer these negative consequences if you make—or someone on your behalf makes—an offer to the IRS that won't be accepted:

- It takes away your time.

- It adds more to your debt, because interest is still being compounded.

- You still owe the taxes; making an offer doesn't make the debt go away.

- You paid someone to put in an offer they likely knew wouldn't be accepted, and you're out whatever money you paid them. (After all, they did what you paid them to do. They put in an offer; they don't have to care whether the offer had a chance.)

- When your offer fails, an offer mill will want to charge you more for doing the resolution work they should have done in the first place, which is to help you come up with a reasonable payment arrangement with the IRS that you can live with.

Once your offer is rejected, we can enter an appeals process. But the debt would continue to mount while we mess around with an offer we know isn't really reasonable. Overall, 80 percent of OICs are rejected, but I'm batting over a 95 percent success rate. That's because I know what I'm doing. We stop, we figure out through extensive interviews where the client is really at, and we tell them what they're qualified for.

We do all the math upfront. We even dig for details you didn't disclose to us, but that the IRS either already knows or is sure to find. (You can't hide *anything* from the IRS.) That's why the overwhelming majority of the offers we make to the IRS are accepted. When you call *Eagle Tax Resolution,* you're talking to true tax resolution professionals— not to a salesperson whose sole interest is in selling you an "offer project."

But I can't help you unless you're completely honest with me.

WHAT DOES THE IRS CONSIDER WHEN REVIEWING AN OFFER?

It's important to note that everything is a factor. When making an OIC for resolution of your tax case, you have to understand how the IRS thinks. You have to think like they think. When making offers, we evaluate alternatives to collection, wrongful levies, and more.

As a tax resolution expert, I understand how the IRS thinks, how they operate to collect their money, and how committed they are to collecting as much money as they can. I also understand how successful offers must take into consideration each individual's unique situation and present it in a way that is credible and smart. I can't emphasize this enough: No two situations are the same. You have to be knowledgeable about which rules to apply to ensure that your offer gets accepted.

You can't do what worked for someone else and just assume it will work for you. I had a guy tell me we should make the same offer his friend made because his friend's offer was accepted. I told him, "Great. I'm glad his offer was accepted. But your situation is different. We have to make a specific offer that takes into consideration your financial situation and any extenuating circumstances." I further explained that his friend's settlement would be different from his. In his friend's case, his assets were only worth $5,000, which was why he was able to settle for $5,000. The friend had no chance of making more money, so the IRS agreed to the offer. They weren't going to do the same for this new client because he had triple the assets his friend had and much better potential to pay the full debt before the CSED.

NOTHING IS OVERLOOKED

Let's say you've got $5,000 sitting in the stock market. If you owe the IRS money, they want that asset. They're not going to allow you to keep your money and investments. If you have $1,200 in stocks, they'll tell you to sell your stocks and pay them the $1,200. You're not going to get the IRS to agree to a lower amount. It doesn't work like that. The IRS takes offers based on your ability to pay and their ability to collect over the period of the collection statute.

Suppose you have $50.00 left over each month after paying bills. That's $600 a year, and the IRS has eight years to go on the statute. They're going to collect $4,800 from you over the next eight years. So if you give them an offer for $1,200, are they going to accept it? No, but if you offer

$4,800 in a lump sum, they might take that. This is because they have the ability to collect $4,800 from you over the next eight years, so they're going to take the long-term approach rather than accept an offer for less than they know they can get before the CSED.

The IRS will accept a legitimate offer from a taxpayer who's making a good-faith effort to do the best they can with their tax debt. They will accept less than you owe if you just don't have the assets, if you're unemployed, or if there are other extenuating circumstances. There are always unique considerations—that's the reality—so you have to look closely at every individual case.

WHO QUALIFIES FOR AN OIC? WHO DOESN'T?

Not everybody qualifies for an OIC. Not everybody qualifies for a resolution plan. I mean, that's the reality of it, right? Not everybody is going to get their offer accepted.

Do you have $100,000 in equity in your home? You owe $30,000 in debt. Guess what? You're not qualified for an offer, because the IRS values your home at 80 percent of its value. If you have a home that's worth $500,000, 80 percent of its value is $400,000. So $400,000 is the value of your home, and let's say you owe $300,000 on it. According to the IRS, you have $100,000 in equity. They would want you to refinance your home and pay off your tax debt.

To determine whether an offer may be accepted, you have to look at reason and the ability for the IRS to collect. Let's say you owe $20,000 or $30,000. You have $100,000 equity in your home. The chances of you selling your home within the next ten years is pretty high. So they would put a lien on it, and when you sell it, they would get their money.

By the way, you're going to pay current market interest. Right now it's 7 percent, so you're going to pay fairly high penalties that will keep increasing. If you start off owing $30,000, by the time you sell your house five years from now, you might owe $45,000, and they're going to take it all.

So at this point, we look at what other options we have. We evaluate:

- Your income

- Your housing, food and utility needs

- Your remaining funds after we apply the IRS's standards of living. (The IRS publishes these for every state and county based on how many people live in your house. If you exceed the standard, they believe that you're living above your means.)

Consider this: You're living a $300,000 life-style, and you owe $100,000 to the IRS. Are they going to accept an offer? I talked with a lady the other day who owed $10 million. So I said, "Tell me about your expenses. What have you got going on?" The first thing she told me was that she has a $10,000 monthly mortgage payment. The IRS standard for her area is $3,000, so she's over by $7,000 per month already. We're not going to get a waiver for her. Her offer will most likely be denied.

Do you know the IRS standard allowances for your area? If you aren't in the tax resolution business, it's unlikely you're as familiar as you need to be with this aspect of the game's rulebook. Let's use Orange County, California, as an example. The housing standard there is $3,032 per month for one person. But let's say you are in a wheelchair. You have to have certain accommodations. You have to live close to the hospital. Under such circumstances, I can make a case to the IRS that justifies why you need to go above the standard housing allowance.

If you don't have extenuating factors, the established standards are as much as you're going to get. In Orange County, you'll get no more than $3,032 per month for your housing. Currently, the ownership cost for a car payment is $629. To create a realistic offer, you calculate your income versus the standards to determine how much is left over every month.

At the end of the month, if you've got $500 left over, multiply $500 by twelve and that is your minimum offer amount for income. Then we take into consideration your assets. You've got $25,000 sitting in an IRA, but you can only withdraw $12,000 because of the rules. So $12,000 now goes into your offer, less the estimated taxes and penalties for a total of about $9,000–$10,800, depending on your tax bracket.

Your income plus your assets create your offer. You've got five cars? You're allowed one. You've got four classic automobiles sitting in your garage? Guess what? The value of those vehicles counts towards your offer.

You don't get to have extra fun stuff if you owe the IRS money. Just because you're broke on paper doesn't mean you're actually broke. To the IRS, it means you're living above your means.

You're living a great lifestyle. You are able to pay your tax debt and move on with life. We can help you no matter what because if you decide to sell one of those cars and pay your tax debt, we can come in on the back side and get certain penalties with their related interest abated.

PAYMENT PLANS

If your reasonable offer is beyond what you feel capable of paying, let's get you on a payment plan. We can pay it all off within a certain amount of time. We can then go back and try to get penalties relieved.

When we work to get a payment plan for our clients, we don't take the regular plan offered by the IRS: the total amount owed, evenly divided over thirty-six months. We work to get a lower and more manageable monthly payment by spreading the repayment over a longer period of time. According to statute, the IRS has 10 years to collect money owed (barring exceptions), starting from the date the tax return is filed.

For example, say the tax return was filed three years ago. There are still seven years remaining, and we can get the payment plan spread across all seven of those years.

I'm working with a client right now who thought she was going to get an offer. She owed about $150,000. After talking to her and realizing she and her husband made over $300,000 a year, I told her she wasn't qualified for an offer, but that I could help them manage their budget. I set them up on a $100 per month payment plan for the first twelve months, and then we jumped to $250 for the next twelve, and so on. This was the arrangement this couple could live with. But it bears repeating: Every case is different.

There are different types of payment plans. There is one that pays off in seventy-two months (that's what you usually get if you call the IRS yourself). In another type, we can extend the debt out to the Collection Statute Expiration Date (CSED), and this will result in a lower payment to help you manage your money. In either of these cases, we can negotiate an agreement where you pay less in the first years and more later. The last and most favorable payment plan is where you do not qualify for an offer, but with your current income you cannot afford to pay the debt in full before the CSED. This is called a Partial Payment Installment Agreement (PPIA). We will do financials for you to determine your available income after allowed expenses. Then we will set up an agreement with the IRS, and if you file on time and do not create more tax debt, then you can stay on this undisturbed until the collection statute expires and you have not paid the full amount. The PPIA is the new offer in compromise because people have equity in their homes. We can guide you through all of this and determine the best resolution option for you.

We're not just here for people who are broke and for whom we can do OICs. We're here for anyone we can help. If you have a high income—great! We can work with you. We can help you manage your cash flow. If you have extra money, you can throw it at the IRS, but you're not required to make that high payment every month. We can set it at a low level for the first few years and let you decide how you want to manage it so you have control. We can argue that with a low payment plan, you can retain investments such as stocks, and when those investments increase in value, you can sell them and pay off your debt. As long as a clear case for fair resolution is made to the IRS, they are inclined to work with you.

We can help clear up everything and reduce your penalties. I had a client who had a $3 million tax bill every year and hadn't filed in multiple years. We went in and wiped out his penalties for the first year—$524,000 gone, just like that! We're not just here to help with small tax debt. We're here to help people reduce their fees even if they make a lot of money.

CONCLUSION

HELP IS HERE

CONCLUSION

As a volleyball referee, I work hard to make sure each match is fair to both sides of the net. I know the rules of the sport, inside and out, and I apply them in a way that makes the competition fair and exciting to watch. After all, it would be no fun to sit through a match you knew was "rigged."

As a tax professional, I fix people's tax problems. I can do that from anywhere, and I do because I care about my clients. As long as I have a computer and internet connection, I can work. The key is,

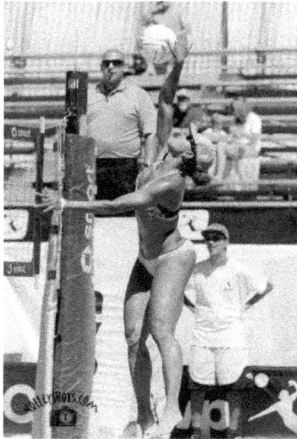

I apply a little bit of a different philosophy in my day job than when I am officiating a volleyball match. Of course I follow the rules to make sure both sides are getting a fair shake—but I am biased for my clients. I know how to use the rules in their favor to save my clients money. I know the rules well enough to make sure that the IRS will accept our resolution plan, because the rulebook says they must.

Allow me to put the rulebook to work for you!

If you've felt overwhelmed by the fear that grips many people who find themselves in tax trouble, don't let that fear rule your life. Give me a call. I have locations in Colorado, California, Texas, and Hawaii. I am federally credentialed, so I can work with you wherever you are located. Most IRS tax resolution work is not done in person.

I can work with you, and the IRS will work with me to help get your tax problem solved, once and for all.

Here's my number:

$$1\text{-}(888)\ \text{EAGLE-}05$$

When you call, rest assured my staff and I will do everything we can to help you.

It will be our honor.

AS A TAX PROFESSIONAL, I FIX PEOPLE'S TAX PROBLEMS.

APPENDICES

- Frequently Asked Questions (FAQs)

- The Taxpayer's Bill of Rights

FREQUENTLY ASKED QUESTIONS (FAQS)

Are Resolution and Compliance the Same Thing?

No. The difference between me and an annual tax filer is this: I deal with resolution, the process by which we fix tax problems. Compliance is once a year; it's the annual filing of your tax return. Tax preparation companies mostly do compliance. With many of these remote companies, you upload your information, they send it to the Philippines or India where they do your tax returns, and when it comes back, they say, "Here, it is done."

A compliance firm will do your tax return, and maybe they do a little tax planning for you or something like that. That's how they're getting involved with your account. But the reality is, their job is solely to do your tax return every year; you see them once annually, they come back with your return, and they charge whatever they charge for this tax prep service.

We don't do compliance. We don't do annual filing. We fix tax problems. That is our specialty. We get referrals from people who take care of annual clients—from CPA offices, other licensed professionals, and sometimes, unlicensed people. We get referrals from these companies because they don't do tax resolution. That's what I do, though, every day, multiple times per day.

What Is a CP 504?

You know you have a levy coming when the IRS sends you a Form CP 504, "Notice of Intent to Levy." In that situation, the IRS is going to take your money, and you're in serious trouble. You have to take substantial action and get the money paid back quickly, or the IRS can and will come after everything they can get. You have thirty days from the date of the letter to do something. Do not wait—call us right away!

Form CP letters are designed to speed up the collection process. These letters are what I deal with on behalf of my clients all the time. Every day, I serve people who are in tax collection status all over the world. State rules differ as to the levy process. For instance, once you get a levy issued in the state of Colorado and they start pulling your wages, you're not going to get that levy released until you have paid your taxes. You have to pay off all of the debt—for that year and whatever year they're going after. They're not going to release your levy just by policy alone. However, if you live in California and you're issued a levy, you may be able to get it suspended. I've gotten many levies revoked. It is possible if your state allows it and if you qualify.

I know what can be done and what can't be done, because I am familiar with different state rules and regulations. That's why a lot of these national companies will not deal with state taxes. They don't want to learn how each state differs. Many tax preparers and so-called resolution experts want to go with a cookie-cutter approach. That's not me, and it's not my firm.

What Is the IRS Fresh Start Program?

The IRS Fresh Start Initiative was created in 2011 to help struggling taxpayers. It is referred to as the Fresh Start Program. It is not a new program and is not a resolution option. It was created to help taxpayers with the limits and give the IRS less strenuous guidelines to follow. I get calls all the time from potential clients who tell me that XYZ firm offered them the Fresh Start Program, and I just smile and figure out what actual IRS resolution option they are able to use. The Fresh Start Program includes Offers in Compromise, Installment Agreements, and Tax Liens.

THE TAXPAYER BILL OF RIGHTS

Here are the rights to which every taxpayer is legitimately entitled:

1 The Right to Be Informed

2 The Right to Quality Service

3 The Right to Pay No More than the Correct Amount of Tax

4 The Right to Challenge the IRS's Position and Be Heard

5 The Right to Appeal an IRS Decision in an Independent Forum

6 The Right to Finality

7 The Right to Privacy

8 The Right to Confidentiality

9 The Right to Retain Representation

10 The Right to a Fair and Just Tax System

ABOUT THE AUTHOR

With more than two decades experience in tax accounting, Joe Aguilar has seen it all. A retired US Marine, Joe takes a no-nonsense approach to helping his clients achieve independence from their tax problems, no matter what it takes.

Joe started by preparing taxes for clients, and quickly realized he could do much more for people who run into tax trouble. Since focusing his practice on tax resolution, Joe has saved millions of dollars for countless delighted clients.

He will not take your tax resolution case if he can't help you.

A former facilitator for the Institute of Internal Auditors, Joe taught the intricacies of auditing to beginners and to management-level professionals. His deep training and experience in auditing give him a unique view into the way auditors think—a key attribute in helping his tax resolution clients work to resolve their problems with the Internal Revenue Service (IRS). He knows how the IRS thinks, and that gives his clients a big advantage.

Joe is your Tax Resolution Referee, stepping between you and the IRS to put your case on a level playing field with the tax man.

A lifelong learner, Joe continues to add to his knowledge base and credentials, which include an MBA and designations as an Enrolled Agent (EA), Certified Internal Auditor (CIA), and Certified Government Auditing Professional (CGAP), as well as a Certification in Control Self-Assessment (CCSA).

Joe's a father of four boys and enjoys travel and riding Harley-Davidsons. His "hobby" as a professional volleyball referee takes him to many parts of the country, and around the world. Joe's unique business model allows him to work from anywhere, so he's always available for you.

www.ingramcontent.com/pod-product-compliance
Lightning Source LLC
Chambersburg PA
CBHW030529210326
41597CB00013B/1079